# J.J. ABRAMS

## Director of *Star Wars: The Force Awakens*

Rebecca Felix

Checkerboard
Library

An Imprint of Abdo Publishing
abdopublishing.com

# ABDOPUBLISHING.COM

Published by Abdo Publishing, a division of ABDO, PO Box 398166, Minneapolis, Minnesota 55439. Copyright © 2017 by Abdo Consulting Group, Inc. International copyrights reserved in all countries. No part of this book may be reproduced in any form without written permission from the publisher. Checkerboard Library™ is a trademark and logo of Abdo Publishing.

Printed in the United States of America, North Mankato, Minnesota

062016
092016

Design: Christa Schneider, Mighty Media, Inc.
Production: Mighty Media, Inc.
Editor: Paige Polinsky
Cover Photograph: AP Images
Interior Photographs: AP Images, p. 25; Everett Collection NYC, pp. 11, 23, 29; Getty Images, pp. 5, 18, 27; iStockphoto, p. 21; Shutterstock, pp. 7, 13, 15, 17, 25, 28; Yearbook Library, pp. 9, 28

**Publishers Cataloging-in-Publication Data**

Names: Felix, Rebecca, author.
Title: J. J. Abrams : director of Star Wars : the Force awakens / by Rebecca Felix.
Description: Minneapolis, MN : Abdo Publishing, [2017] | Series: Movie makers |
    Includes index.
Identifiers: LCCN 2016934265 | ISBN 9781680781816 (lib. bdg.) |
    ISBN 9781680775662 (ebook)
Subjects: LCSH: Abrams, J. J. (Jeffrey Jacob), 1966- --Juvenile literature. |
    Motion picture producers and directors--United States--Biography--Juvenile
    literature. | Screenwriters--United States--Biography--Juvenile literature.
Classification: DDC 791.4302/33/092 [B]--dc23
LC record available at http://lccn.loc.gov/2016934265

# CONTENTS

# A GREAT FORCE

Long ago, in a **galaxy** far, far away, a war erupts. An evil empire and a rebel army battle on strange planets filled with odd creatures. Huge spaceships race past stars and fire **laser beams**.

This is the world of Star Wars. It is one of the most successful film series of all time! A new **trilogy** of these space films began in 2015. Movie maker J.J. Abrams **directed** the first film.

*Star Wars: The Force Awakens* is the fifth film Abrams has directed. However, he has been involved in many other movies and television shows. Abrams has worked as a writer, **producer**, **composer**, musician, and actor. As of 2015, Abrams has produced more than 600 television **episodes**!

J.J. Abrams attends the premiere of *Star Wars: The Force Awakens* in Hollywood, California. *The Force Awakens* has made more money than any other Star Wars movie.

Abrams is known for creating stories full of mystery and **suspense**. Before *The Force Awakens* was released, fans tried to guess what twists Abrams would bring to the Star Wars story. But he kept them guessing! This talented **director** has enjoyed mystery since childhood.

# CHOOSING
# MYSTERY

Jeffrey Jacobs "J.J." Abrams was born in New York City, New York, on June 27, 1966. He was the son of Gerald and Carol Ann Abrams. J.J. also had a sister named Tracy.

Gerald Abrams worked in the entertainment industry as a **producer**. J.J. spent time with him on movie and television **sets**. This behind-the-**scenes** experience influenced J.J.'s future career. But his greatest inspiration came from a small mystery.

As a boy, J.J. went to a magic store with his grandfather, Henry Kelvin. While there, J.J. bought a mystery box. The box's contents were a surprise. J.J. took the box home. But he never opened it, even to this day!

## FAST FACT

J.J. has named many minor characters in his movies Kelvin, after his grandfather.

Abrams's birthplace, New York City, was also the setting of his 2008 science-fiction film *Cloverfield*.

To J.J., the secrets hidden in the mystery box meant possibility. It made him think about secrets and **suspense**. It also made him compare movies to mysteries. People go to a movie theater not knowing exactly what they will see. The entire experience is a surprise revealed as they watch.

# CHAPTER 3

# SUPER 8 FILMS

When J.J. was young, his family moved to Los Angeles, California. Carol sold homes in the area. Gerald worked on several popular television shows in Hollywood. J.J. often spent time on **set** as his father worked.

J.J. was ten years old when his grandfather bought him a **super 8mm** camera. J.J. began making his own short films. They often featured monsters, battles, and chase **scenes**. J.J. made **props** and costumes out of whatever he could find. His friends and older sister acted in the films.

## BRIGHT IDEA

When he was 15, J.J. went to a movie screening. It was for *Escape from New York*, a film Gerald produced. Afterward, J.J. suggested a change to the filmmakers. His idea made it into the final movie!

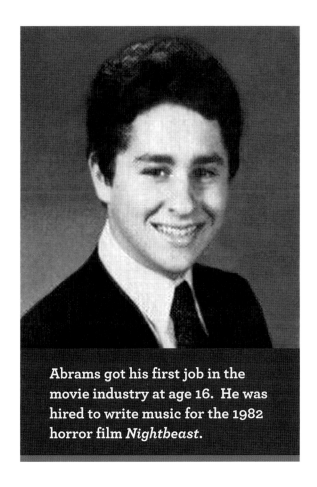

Abrams got his first job in the movie industry at age 16. He was hired to write music for the 1982 horror film *Nightbeast*.

At age 15, J.J. entered The Best Teen **Super 8mm** Films of '81. The film festival took place in Los Angeles. J.J.'s friend Matt Reeves also entered a film. Neither teen won. But a local newspaper interviewed them about their work.

Famous **director** Steven Spielberg read that article. He was impressed by J.J. and Matt's talent. Spielberg hired the pair to restore his own early 8mm films. J.J. was thrilled to work for his moviemaking hero. And it would not be the last time they worked together.

# SCREENPLAY SUCCESS

# CHAPTER 4

In 1984, Abrams graduated from Palisades Charter High School in Los Angeles. He then moved back to New York. There, he attended Sarah Lawrence College in Yonkers.

At Sarah Lawrence, Abrams studied to get his **liberal arts** degree. He also wrote **screenplays** in his spare time. Before graduating in 1988, Abrams co-wrote a screenplay with a fellow student. To the pair's surprise, it was purchased and made into a movie. The screenplay became 1990's *Taking Care of Business*.

After *Taking Care of Business*, Abrams's career was set in motion. He wrote screenplays for several more films. These include *Regarding Henry*, released in 1991, and 1992's *Forever Young*. The films weren't very popular among **critics**. But they marked the start of Abrams's career in the film industry.

In *Regarding Henry*, Harrison Ford (*left*) plays an ambitious lawyer who has lost his memory.

In 1994, a friend introduced Abrams to a woman named Katie McGrath. Abrams and McGrath, a **public relations** executive, began dating. Two years later, they were married. McGrath would later work with Abrams as a story editor.

In 1998, Abrams and McGrath's first son, Henry, was born. Later that year, *Armageddon* was released. It is a science-fiction adventure film based on Abrams's **screenplay**. Despite mixed reviews, *Armageddon* was the top-selling film during its opening week. Its action-packed story was unlike anything Abrams had ever created.

That same year, the first season of college drama *Felicity* aired on television. Abrams co-wrote the show with his childhood friend Reeves. *Felicity* was very popular, especially with its female viewers. The show won several awards, including a **Golden Globe Award** for Best TV Series Drama. The series was just the beginning of Abrams's success in television.

FAST FACT

Felicity, played by actor Keri Russell, had very long, curly hair. When Russell cut her hair short, the show's ratings dropped.

McGrath (*left*) and Abrams attend a theater opening in Westwood, California. McGrath loves to tease Abrams about "his crazy secrecy stuff."

# TV MYSTERIES

## SECRET STUDIO

Abrams's studio headquarters reflects his love of mystery. Its name, Bad Robot Productions, is not on the building. Instead the sign mysteriously says National Typewriter Co. Inside, Abrams's bathroom is hidden behind a secret wall. It can only be entered by pulling a certain book off the shelf!

The late 1990s brought many changes for Abrams. In 1998, he co-founded a production company called Bad Robot Productions. His daughter, Gracie, was born in 1999.

That same year, Abrams wrote and **produced** a new television series called *Alias*. Its main character, Sydney, is a spy working as a **double agent**. Abrams was inspired by the popular spy film series Mission: Impossible.

Abrams (*center*) and the cast of *Alias* at the 2002 book release of *Alias: Declassified: The Official Companion*. The book gives a behind-the-scenes look at the television show.

*Alias* features the **suspense** and mystery Abrams loves. **Critics** seemed to love it too. Although it was never considered a commercial hit, it gained a devoted group of fans.

*Alias* ran until 2006. In its fourth season, Abrams began yet another show. That show, *Lost*, remains unlike any other in television history.

*Lost*'s **pilot** was released in 2004. Abrams wrote and **directed** the two-part **episode**. Its opening **scene** is a good example of Abrams's style. It pulls viewers in with its mystery and **suspense**.

The scene begins with a smoking, twisted airplane. It seems that the plane has crashed on an island. Later episodes reveal many exciting twists and turns. Fans could not get enough. *Lost* immediately became a major success.

*Lost* aired for six years. It has been called Abrams's best work. One writer compared the show to Abrams's own mystery box. As soon as viewers thought they had an answer, new questions would emerge. Fans were kept guessing about the mysterious island until the final episode in 2010.

During its run, *Lost*, its actors and crew, and Abrams were nominated for hundreds of awards. It won 84 of them, including Abrams's 2005 **Emmy Award**. The Emmy was awarded for Outstanding Directing for a Drama Series.

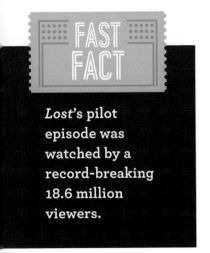

FAST FACT

*Lost*'s pilot episode was watched by a record-breaking 18.6 million viewers.

# CRITICS REACT

"Abrams is also. . . behind some of the best television series of the past two **decades**. . . [*Lost*] fully cemented Abrams as a TV genius. It was a serious, adult mystery, full of twists and turns that still to this day **infuriates** and delights **legions** of fans."

—Paul Harris,
*The Guardian*

"Once upon a time, there was a television show about a bunch of people on an island. For six years it was one of the most fascinating things on TV. And then it ended, in the worst way possible. *Lost* ended tonight, and with it the hopes and dreams of millions of people who thought it might finally get good again. SPOILER ALERT: It didn't."

—Max Read,
*Gawker*

Both of these writers critique Abrams's work on *Lost*. Although one review is negative and one is positive, how are these quotes similar?

# MAN ON A MISSION

Abrams received many awards for *Alias* and *Lost*. Meanwhile, his Hollywood peers began to notice his talent. These included actor Tom Cruise, the star of the Mission: Impossible films.

Cruise was impressed by Abrams's work on *Lost* and *Alias*. He wanted Abrams to **direct** the third Mission: Impossible film. Abrams could hardly believe it. Cruise's spy films had always inspired Abrams. Now Abrams would have a chance to make a Mission: Impossible movie of his own!

*Mission: Impossible III* was Abrams's first time directing a full-length film. He also helped write the **script**. When the movie was released in 2006, it was a hit. The film made $16.6 million on its first day alone. Six weeks after its release, *Mission: Impossible III* remained one of the most successful films in theaters.

Abrams (*second from left*) poses with part of the *Mission: Impossible III* team, including actor Tom Cruise (*center*). The group traveled to Tokyo to attend the film's Japanese premiere in 2006.

Cruise said Abrams brought great characters, storytelling, and tension to the film. Years later, Abrams would **direct** films for two of the most beloved series of all time. Both would take Abrams on journeys out of this world.

# GALACTIC TAKEOVER

CHAPTER

7

As Abrams's career grew busier, his family grew larger. His and McGrath's son August was born in January 2006. By July, Abrams was scheduled to **direct** another major movie. The film was a **reboot** of the classic space television series *Star Trek*.

Fans and **critics** alike were delighted when *Star Trek* was released in 2009. It was the highest-earning Star Trek movie of all time. In 2011, Abrams was hired to direct the film's **sequel**.

Abrams was finishing *Star Trek Into Darkness* when he received a call from Lucasfilm. Lucasfilm was the production company created by Star Wars creator George Lucas. The Walt Disney Company had recently bought Lucasfilm and announced the production of a new Star Wars movie. To Abrams's surprise, he was asked to direct the film.

Abrams directs actor Chris Pine on the set of *Star Trek*.
Pine plays James Kirk, captain of the starship *Enterprise*.

Although Abrams was a huge Star Wars fan, he turned the job down. **Directing** a film in this legendary series was too much pressure. But McGrath encouraged him to change his mind. So, Abrams began his journey into the Star Wars world.

# ON THE SET OF
# STAR WARS: THE FORCE AWAKENS

The seventh Star Wars movie was filmed in many locations. The crew traveled to Ireland, London, and Abu Dhabi. And in each place, Abrams kept busy!

As **director**, Abrams organized everything on **set** to create his vision for the film. He was also in charge of solving problems. One problem proved dangerous for Abrams.

Harrison Ford plays Han Solo, one of the lead **roles** in *Star Wars: The Force Awakens*. While filming in 2014, a door fell off the spaceship *Millennium Falcon*. It landed on Ford, breaking his ankle and trapping him. Abrams rushed to help. But while lifting the door, Abrams broke his back!

## FAST FACT

Abrams worked with the Walt Disney Company to create Force for Change. The charity uses Star Wars to inspire kids worldwide to make healthy choices.

24

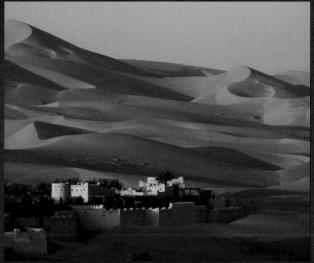

Harrison Ford, Anthony Daniels, Carrie Fisher, and Peter Mayhew acted in the first Star Wars film. They returned to their original roles for Abrams's movie.

The team traveled to the Rub 'al-Khali desert to film scenes set on Jakku. They spent six months filming there.

Abrams had to wear a back brace for the rest of filming. But he was still thrilled to work on a series he had loved since childhood. "That was a constant in the production of the movie: moments where we would all look around and realize what we were doing and gasp a little bit and then dive back in," Abrams said.

Star Wars fans young and old were excited to see Abrams's addition to the series. The movie earned more than $100 million in pre-order ticket sales. When it was released in December of 2015, it was a massive hit. More than 28 million tickets were sold during its first weekend in theaters!

*The Force Awakens* shattered many records. In just 12 days, it became the fastest movie to earn $1 billion in theaters. Soon after, it became the highest-earning US film ever made. Star Wars fans and **critics** had varying reactions. But most were happy with Abrams's extension of the space **saga**.

Today, Abrams lives in Pacific Palisades, California, with his family. He is working on several movies, including the next Star Wars film. Abrams is its executive **producer**. As for what other projects await this talented movie maker? It's anyone's guess. But don't expect Abrams to tell!

## SPACE DRAMA

During interviews, Abrams said he was a bigger fan of Star Wars than Star Trek. This made many Star Trek fans furious. Some fans and critics questioned whether it was wise for Abrams to direct films for both series. They feared he may mix up important details.

Abrams promotes *Star Wars: The Force Awakens* at the largest Disney fan convention, D23 EXPO, in Anaheim, California.

# TIMELINE

### 1966
Jeffrey Jacob "J.J." Abrams is born on June 27.

### 1970s
Abrams buys a mystery box. It inspires him throughout his career.

### 1988
Abrams graduates from Sarah Lawrence College.

### 1990
*Taking Care of Business* is released. It is Abrams's first project to become a full-length film.

### 1996
Abrams and Katie McGrath are married.

### 1998
Abrams's son, Henry, is born. Abrams cofounds Bad Robot Productions.

# FAMOUS WORKS

### Felicity
1998–2002

Felicity attends the fictional University of New York (UNY).

Nominated: Best TV Series–Drama, Golden Globe Awards, 1999

### Alias
2001–2006

Abrams wrote and performed the song that plays during the show's opening credits.

Won: TV Program of the Year, AFI Awards, 2004

### Lost
2004–2010

Extreme fans of the show call themselves Losties or Lostaways.

Won: Best TV Series–Drama, Golden Globe Awards, 2006

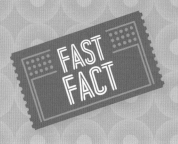
J.J.'s company, Bad Robot Productions, created and sold its own mystery box! But its contents were not a complete surprise. The boxes held a card game.

**1999**
Abrams and McGrath's daughter, Gracie, is born.

**2004**
*Lost*'s record-breaking pilot premieres on television.

**2005**
*Lost* wins Abrams an Emmy for Outstanding Directing for a Drama Series.

**2006**
Abrams's son August is born. *Mission Impossible III* is released.

**2009**
Abrams's *Star Trek* is released. It is the highest-earning film in the series.

**2015**
*The Force Awakens* is released. It becomes the highest-earning US film ever made.

### Mission Impossible: III
Released 2006

Actor Tom Cruise did most of his own stunts for the film.

Won: Top Box Office Films, ASCAP Film and Television Music Awards, 2007

### Star Trek
Released 2009

Steven Spielberg advised Abrams on some action scenes.

Won: Top Box Office Films, ASCAP Film and Television Music Awards, 2010

### Star Wars: The Force Awakens
Released 2015

Abrams released trading cards to reveal the main characters.

Won: Movie of the Year, AFI Awards, 2016

# GLOSSARY

**composer** – a person who writes music.

**critic** – a professional who gives his or her opinion on art, literature, or performances.

**decade** – a time period of ten years.

**direct** – to supervise people in a play, movie, or television program. Someone who directs is a *director*.

**double agent** – a spy pretending to serve one government while actually serving another.

**Emmy Award** – an award recognizing excellence in the television industry.

**episode** – one of the programs in a television or movie series.

**galaxy** – a very large group of stars and planets. Something from or relating to a galaxy is *galactic*.

**Golden Globe Award** – an award recognizing excellence in both the movie and television industries.

**infuriate** – to make someone extremely angry.

**laser beam** – a very narrow, intense beam of light that can be used for cutting things.

**legion** – a very large number.

**liberal arts** – areas of study, such as history and literature, meant to provide general knowledge rather than to develop specific career skills.

**pilot** – a television episode created as a sample of a proposed series.

**produce** – to oversee staff and funding to put on a play or make a movie or TV show. Someone who produces is a *producer*.

**prop** – any item other than costumes or furniture that appears in a play, movie, or television show.

**public relations** – the methods or activities an organization or a business uses to promote goodwill or a good image with the public.

**reboot** – to make new versions or episodes of a movie or TV series after a long break.

**role** – an actor's part in a play, movie, or TV show.

**saga** – a long, complicated story.

**scene** – a part of a play, movie, or TV show that presents what is happening in one particular place and time.

**screening** – an event in which a movie is shown to a group of viewers.

**screenplay** – the written form of a story prepared for a movie.

**script** – the written words and directions used to put on a play, movie, or television show.

**sequel** (SEE-kwuhl) – a book, movie, or other work that continues the story begun in a preceding one.

**set** – an artificial setting where a play is performed or a movie or television program is filmed.

**super 8mm** – a film format used in a type of home movie camera.

**suspense** – an anxious and uncertain feeling caused by not knowing what might happen next.

**trilogy** – a series of three novels, movies, or other works that are closely related and involve the same characters or themes.

# INDEX